O'ahu

IMAGES OF THE GATHERING PLACE

Photography by

Douglas Peebles

Mutual Publishing

Library of Congress Catalog Card Number: 2004106191

ISBN-10: 1-56647-670-4
ISBN-13: 978-1-56647-670-6

Tenth Printing, June 2014

Mutual Publishing, LLC
1215 Center Street, Suite 210
Honolulu, Hawai'i 96816
Ph: (808) 732-1709 / Fax: (808) 734-4094
e-mail: info@mutualpublishing.com
www.mutualpublishing.com
Printed in Korea

Gracing the edge of Waikīkī, Diamond Head provides the perfect scenery
to enjoy a hula performance or a day at the beach.

A breathtaking view from the Lanipō Trail in the Koʻolau mountains.

A bird's-eye view of Kāneʻohe Bay reveals the Windward side of Oʻahu.

The Aloha Tower was built in 1926 as a symbol of the Hawaiian Islands, to be remembered by the ships entering and leaving Honolulu Harbor.

Mokulēʻia Beach on the North Shore is one of Oʻahu's most pristine and remote beaches.

The sweeping panorama from Waiāhole Beach Park in Kāneʻohe offers a view
of the Puʻukānehoalani cliffs and a glimpse of Chinaman's Hat to the right.

The Polynesian Cultural Center continues to be a
popular tourist attraction featuring various South
Pacific cultures. PHOTO COURTESY OF THE POLYNESIAN CULTURAL CENTER

The Mormon Temple, established in the early 1900s, sits against the backdrop of the Koʻolau Mountains, reflecting crisp blue skies in its pool. PHOTO COURTESY OF THE POLYNESIAN CULTURAL CENTER

A surfer in the Eddie Aikau Contest rides a majestic wave on the North Shore.

Makapuʻu Lighthouse welcomes many ships
sailing into Honolulu from the West.

Hoʻomaluhia Park, a botanical garden luxuriously sprawled at the base
of the Kāneʻohe cliffs, offers a quiet escape from city life.

Teeming with unusual fishes, the crescent shores of Hanauma Bay is a popular recreational spot for swimming and snorkeling on Oʻahu.

A typically beautiful, sunny day peeks through the cliffs
of the historical Nuʻuanu Pali Lookout.

Diamond Head, Hawai'i's most well-known landmark, rises up from the sea with Kapi'olani Park at its base and Waikīkī highrises stretching into the distance.

Waimea Bay on a calm day offers families a fun-filled outing at the beach.

The sunset at Kawela Bay veils the ocean with its celestial palette of pink and orange light.

A humpback whale breaches off Kāneʻohe.

Known for its tranquil surroundings, world-class resort and spa, the
beautiful Koʻolina coast of west Oʻahu is one of the best
places to relax and enjoy paradise.

Punchbowl Crater, also known as Pūowaina, is home to the
National Memorial Cemetery of the Pacific.

In ancient Hawaiian times, Kualoa was considered one of the
most sacred places on the island.

This daytime view of Honolulu city captures Ala Moana Beach Park, the ʻIlikai Yacht Harbor and the urban sprawl below the Koʻolau Mountains.

A surfer comes in from Magic Island.

The peaks of Olomana stand tall against the clear shores of Kailua.

Built in 1968, the Byodo-in Temple at Valley of the Temples Memorial Park in Kahalu'u is a replica of a famous Kyoto Temple that houses a three-ton bronze bell and an 18 foot-high Buddha.

Hālona Beach, a quiet patch of sand at the base of the Hālona Blowhole,
is best known for the famous movie scene in *From Here to Eternity*.

Young hula dancers perform a kahiko, an ancient hula.

Canoes rest peacefully near Chinaman's Hat.

A drive through Wahiawā is lined with endless pineapple fields.

The USS *Arizona* Memorial honors the lives lost during the attack on Pearl Harbor in World War II.

The statue of Duke Kahanamoku stands
along the shore of Waikīkī,

An aerial view of Ka'ena Point captures high surfs of twenty feet crashing inland.

The mountains and ocean meet in panoramic harmony at Kailua Bay.

Sunlight accentuates the sculpted ridges of the Koʻolau Mountains.

An endangered species protected by federal and state laws, the green sea turtle
can often be seen swimming in the clear waters of the Pacific.

A rainbow glows in Nuʻuanu Valley after misty showers.

Built in 1925 on Honolulu's Waterfront, Aloha Tower
was patterned after San Francisco's Ferry Building.

The *Hōkūleʻa*, one of Hawaiʻi's most famous voyaging vessels, is at home on the sea.

With the Kāneʻohe cliffs behind her, a hula dancer
gestures towards the sky.

The rising moon lights a path across the ocean between
the Mokulua Islands— nicknamed the Mokes.

Sandy Beach is one of the most challenging bodysurfing spots on O‘ahu.

Diamond Head and Waikīkī shimmer in the early
evening light shortly after sunset.